T0065415

A SPIRITUAL UPLIFTING

POEMS OF INSPIRATION AND ENCOURAGEMENT

DORRIS OWNEY JACKSON

authorHOUSE®

AuthorHouse™
1663 Liberty Drive
Bloomington, IN 47403
www.authorhouse.com
Phone: 833-262-8899

Published by AuthorHouse 02/11/2021

ISBN: 978-1-6655-1693-8 (sc)
ISBN: 978-1-6655-1694-5 (e)

Library of Congress Control Number: 2021902868

Print information available on the last page.

Any people depicted in stock imagery provided by Getty Images are models, and such images are being used for illustrative purposes only. Certain stock imagery © Getty Images.

This book is printed on acid-free paper.

DEDICATION

In loving memory of my Mom and Dad
Maggie and Samuel Owney Sr.
Who instilled the love of God in me
Who taught me to love in spite of.
To always trust and believe that
God can, will and does. Because he is love

His Spirit abides in me
My Spirit abides in him

ACKNOWLEDGMENTS

All praise, honor, and glory to my Lord and Savior Jesus Christ, for giving me life and insight, wisdom and knowledge to write and a heart to share.

To my sister Essie Peterson Johnson (RIP)
Who was my mom away from home.
Who taught me to face issues and obstacles head on.

To my brother Herman Heard who always provides an ear to hear and a voice of encouragement.

Dorris Owney Jackson

GOD SENDS ANGELS

GOD SENDS ANGELS TO WATCH OVER US.
IN THIS LIFE ON EARTH IT'S CERTAINLY A PLUS.

THEY LEAD AND GUIDE US ON OUR DAILY WALK.
WE DON'T ALWAYS RECOGNIZE THEM
EVEN THOUGH THEY TALK.

THEY DON'T COME DRESSED IN WHITE.
AS SOME THINK THEY MIGHT.

THEY DON'T HAVE LARGE FEATHERED WINGS.
FLY THROUGH THE AIR OR ANY OF THOSE THINGS.

THEY SIMPLY MAY BE A STRONG SENSATION.
TO HELP US FACE SOME REALIZATIONS.

WE MAY NOT OTHERWISE HAVE SEEN.
I HOPE YOU UNDERSTAND WHAT I MEAN.

THEY MAY EVEN COME IN AN EARTHLY FORM.
PROTECTING US FROM DANGER AND HARM.

ASSISTING US WITH ALL OUR NEEDS.
JUST FOLLOW THEM AND TAKE THEIR LEAD.

THEIR ORDERS COME FROM HEAVEN ABOVE.
OUR FATHER DIRECTING THEM WITH HIS LOVE.

MUSTARD SEED FAITH

To have a little Faith in God.
You reap rewards forever large.

Belief, loyalty, obligation <u>to</u> him.
Security, protection, grace and mercy <u>from</u> him.

All these things you shall enjoy.
Pain and suffering will be no more.

Confidence and trust, place it in the Lord.
Bestow faithfulness, praise on your own accord.

Live in harmony within his word.
Retreat from worldly sin unto him serve.

Listen patiently and hear his voice.
He gives us all this wonderful choice.

"Choose ye this day whom you will serve."
As for me and my house we will serve the Lord.

I MUST WORK

I MUST WORK THE WORKS OF HIM THAT SENT ME WHILE IT IS DAY.

I MUST WORK TO SHOW MYSELF APPROVED.
THE BIBLE IS MY REFUGE, MY DAILY GUIDE, MY FOOD

I MUST WORK, GOD GIVES ME STRENGTH AND POWER. HE IS MY FATHER, MY FRIEND, MY STRONG TOWER.

I MUST WORK AND BE NOT ASHAMED.
I AM HIS WORKMANSHIP CREATED IN CHRIST JESUS NAME.

I MUST WORK AND WORSHIP THEE.
THE LORD'S BEEN GOOD TO ME.

I MUST WORK TO KEEP HIS COMMANDMENTS.
AND ABIDE IN HIS LOVE. ETERNAL LIFE MY REWARD
FOREVER WITH MY FATHER ABOVE.

THE NIGHT COMETH WHEN NO MAN CAN WORK.
A CHANCE LIKE THAT I DARE NOT TAKE.

MADE TO HONOR HIM

Thou art worthy, O Lord of honor, glory and power.
I live to praise your name every minute of every hour.

For thou has created all things for thy pleasure.
Rewarded unto man, blessings of great measure.

From the windows of heaven above.
Comes the promise of protection, comfort and love.

I give Godly sorrow in repentance to salvation.
Unto the Lord, I come with visions of revelation.

He that hath an ear let him hear.
The presence of God is ever near.

He knows our works and where we dwell.
Through worship and prayer all is well.

Lord, I give you hallelujah praise.
Now and for the rest of my days.

BECAUSE

Because you are a child of God.
Life on earth sometimes get hard.

But, God promised in his word.
And I'm very sure you've heard.

I'll never leave or forsake you he said.
You have no need to be afraid

Trials and tribulations yes, they will come.
Lots for a few, less for some.

No matter what you may go through.
God is the answer and this is true.

His grace is sufficient to guide the way.
If on the lighted path you stay.

There may be times when you may fall.
Right there he'll be to answer your call.

To give you strength and make you strong.
Because of him you can't go wrong.

So, know that until the very end
In Christ you have a father and friend.

SOMETHING HAPPENED

A major change has come about.
I feel the urge to jump and shout.

A peaceful calm has come over me.
God worked a miracle for all to see.

I like the feeling it gives within.
Adds excitement where sadness has been.

He always keeps a watchful eye.
My Lord, my Savior, my private spy.

Making sure I'm safe and my mind is clear.
I keep him close always near.
No longer that unknown fear.

That kept me sad and bound.
As though he wasn't around.

This gift I wish for everyone.
So open your heart and let him come.

STRONG FAITH
STRONG FINISH

My Faith is Stong
He forgives my wrongs
He never leaves me alone

Lifes journey is not easy
And that is the reason
To trust God in every season

No night or day is ever the same
Whether it be sunshine or rain

God is there to guide the way
If on the righteous path you stay

This earthly journey is just the beginning
My Faith is Strong from start to finish

I LOVE TO PRAISE HIM

Praising God is what I do.
I hope you love to praise him to.

He made us all just for this cause.
To lift his name above it all.

Obedience is the key to righteousness.
We must be strong to pass the test.
Only then will we be blessed.

He gave his only son to die.
To give to us eternal life.

Do we deserve it, no we don't.
But, God is master, it's what he wants.

His love is eternal, never ending.
We never lose, always winning.

Jesus loves us this we know.
He shows us daily as we grow.

Into understanding and repentance.
Open doors and open windows.

GOING THROUGH DARK PLACES

There are seeds in you.
That would not come through.

If they were not in a dark place.
It's a necessary space.

In the dark places you are being blessed.
Even though it's sure to cause distress.

When you go through a few dark places.
That's when you learn how to pray.

It's then you develope spiritual muscle.
In God you began to trust.

The dark places are a part of the plan.
So God can make you into only what he..can.

You have to go through, this you must know.
Only then the seeds planted will grow.

REST DON'T STRESS

When in a state of rest.
Out comes your very best.

So take the time to meditate.
Then patiently wait for something great.

Mind, body and soul at peace.
Praying it will never cease.

A quiet calm full of joy.
Endless, lasting forever more.

Nothing is impossible, if only you believe.
Gently, trusting, easily conceived.

A peaceful journey happily received.
Simply because you believed.

No grief, no fear, no pain.
All else would be in vain.

Rest don't stress.
Out will come your very best.

I WON'T GO BACK

The doctor can operate.
But, God can heal.

When I stumble and I fall.
I feel my fathers touch.

He lifts me up and paves the way.
Start over my child I hear him say.

It will be alright.
I am here, you're never alone.

No matter how dark it might seem.
You're safely in my arms, its not a dream.

To know this I feel safe and secure.
That my father is ever near.
I won't go back.

SHADES OF GRAY

If its God you're after.
You have to choose one master.

You can't straddle the fence.
No matter what you meant.

It has to be white or black.
It just doesn't work like that.

Be consistent in your faith.
Even if he makes you wait.

Everything he does, in his own time.
This you need to keep in mind.

If it's God you're after.
You have to choose one master.

CHECK YOURSELF

Check yourself.
Don't wreck yourself.

Look in the mirror now and then.
Remember in God you have a friend.

To lead and guide you on your way.
If in his presence you choose to stay.

Spend time with him in daily prayer.
He promised to be with you everywhere.

He will give you peace and joy.
Grace and mercy in overflow.
So go and sin no more.

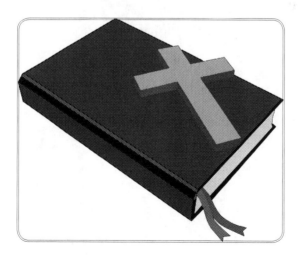

DON'T BOND OVER BAGGAGE

Don't bond over baggage
It's a really bad habit

You will never get to know and see
The person you've met and who they could be

Leave your old you in the past
To find a relationship that will last

Vow not to make the same mistakes
Listen, learn and wait, don't haste

True love is worth the wait
To end up with the perfect mate

Patience will bring that one of a kind
Then you can say this one is mine

I AM HERE

You may not see me
But, I am here

Always with you
Always near

Listen closely
And you will hear
My voice soft and clear

I will pull away all the weeds
And provide to you all you need

Because I promised, you are my seed
Ask of me you shall receive

Then you can spread your wings
And be blessed with everything

WITH OPEN ARMS

Like an angel I spread my wings I fly
Like an angel I will live beyond the sky

Like an angel I will have eternal life
No more problems, sickness or strife

Praising my father both day and night
No more darkness just shiny and light

Sounds of trumpets, cymbals, and drums
No aging or diseases everyone young

My father sitting on the throne
Jesus beside him never alone

Friends and loved ones will be there
Loving each other not one little care

Laughing, singing, dancing, always something to do
Living happily together, waiting for you

"WHEN IT HURTS"

Sitting at home alone in pain
So bad, about to go insane

Piercing, throbbing holding my head
Sobbing, doubting my God's holy word
Call upon the elders, I remember he said

Picked up the telephone made a call
She started to pray, God won't let you fall

Lord ease her pain and calm her spirit
Please touch her Father do it now
You are the only one who knows just how

Help her believe she's not alone
Because you are with her in her home

Read these scriptures I give you daughter
Psalm 38 so you won't falter

Started to read and write them down
So much relief, no longer a frown

Pain relieved, suddenly gone
Thank you Jesus no longer alone

"GOD CAN"

God can do anything but fail.
I'm a living witness with lots to tell.

He woke me up this morning, started me on my way.
I praise and thank him at the beginning and end of each day.

I thank him for posting his angels to watch over me.
Satan keeps trying to trick me, but God makes him flee.

He gave his only son that I might live.
Prosperity, a good life for me, is his will.

Oh, how I love him. I want you to know.
And in his wisdom I continue to grow.

The only thing he asks in return.
Obedience, praise, and love for my fellow man.

Without my father, where would I be.
I pray in this life to never see.

One day I'll meet him face to face.
In the mean time he gives me mercy and grace.

If I had ten thousand tongues. I couldn't thank him enough.
So, on this christian journey, I'll keep traveling I must.

IF* IT* IS* TO* BE

If it is to be.
It is up to me.

To invest my time.
And my mind.

In positive things.
Accomplished dreams

If it is to be.
It is up to me.

To pave the road.
Then set my goals.

Within my reach they are.
More near than far.

If it is to be.
It is up to me

Like an eagle with wings I soar.
Happy, content with so much joy.

If it is to be.
It is up to me.

THE DEPTH OF THE SEA

IN THE DEPTH OF THE SEA
GOD PLACES FORGIVEN SINS

JUST ASK FOR YOURS TO GO THERE
THEN EVERYBODY WINS

NO MATTER IF ITS FRIENDS, FOE, OR KIN
IN THE DEPTH OF THE SEA SIN CAN END

A NEW BEGINNING A NEW LIFE
NO LONGER FILLED WITH SIN AND STRIFE

GOD CREATES IN YOU A CLEAN SPIRIT
OPEN YOUR EYES AND EARS TO HEAR IT

SEEK AND YE SHALL FIND
GODS DELIVERANCE AND PEACE OF MIND

GOD SPOKE

God spoke and things began to appear

God spoke and there came light, sky, and earth

God spoke vegetation and plants that yielded seed

God spoke and trees beared fruit

God spoke the sun, moon and stars shined

God spoke and there appeared water, fish and birds

God spoke and there appeared every kind of living creature
livestock, wild and domestic beast

God spoke, earth was created and everything in it
from nothing, upheld by nothing, that can be seen was spoken

HE (GOD) PROMISED

When times are rough.
You feel you've had enough.

Lean on Jesus.
He's here to relieve us.

I'll never leave or forsake you he said.
It's written in the bible God's holy word.

Just ask in prayer believing.
His promise is that of receiving.

Whatever is needed, comes right on time.
To strengthen your body, soul, and mind.

Never doubt his promises simply trust and obey.
Be patient and wait for help to come your way.

Give God his time each and every day.
Miracles and blessings will continually come your way.

Try him and you will see.
Open your eyes and look at me.

VENT IT AWAY-PRAY

Speak to your situation
Not about it, procrastinating

Don't be ashamed
Pray in Jesus name

Believe God's word
Everything he said

Ask, it shall be given you
Only if your heart is true

He knows evil and deception
Truth and dedication

Life not death
Equals eternal rest

LONELINESS

Lord, why do I sometimes feel so alone?
With family members living in my home.
Something is missing in my life.
I know I'm a good person, mother and wife.
I strive to help others as much as I can.
And Lord I keep you always in my plan.
You have the answers I seek to find.
Place them somewhere within my mind.
You put no burdens on me that I can't bear.
Relief is coming soon, I just don't know when or where.
You said in your word ask, believe*** and we shall recieve.
You allowed your son Jesus to die on the cross.
So that, I and all others would not be lost.
With this in mind I walk by Faith.
Patiently waiting and abiding in your Grace.

NO GRACE LAND

NO GRACE LAND
NEVER IN MY PLAN

NOT EVER GOING TO THAT PLACE
A LAND OF SHAME AND DISGRACE

HE FORGAVE ALL THE MISTAKES THAT I MADE
NOW, I LIVE HAPPY CONTENT AND SAVED

I MAY HAVE SLIPS AND DOWNFALLS
BUT, GOD LIVES ON THE INSIDE OF MY FOUR WALLS

HE WALKS WITH ME AND TALKS WITH ME
I'M OPEN AND HONEST FOR ALL TO SEE

THERE WAS A TIME I TRIED TO FLEE
NO LONGER, BECAUSE NOW I AM FREE

TO DO HIS WILL AND GIVE HIM PRAISE
NOW AND FOR THE REST OF MY DAYS

I UNDERSTAND AMAZING GRACE
HE GIVES IT TO ME IN EVERYTHING I FACE

~WHEN IT'S HARD TO TRUST~

Why is it so hard to trust
The people that we love so much

We open up our hearts in pride
Taking every step in stride

Not thinking their intents aren't true
My Lord if we only knew

It causes us to start and doubt
The smiles, the lies, what are they about

An opportunist, abusing a friend
This really gets under my skin

The only thing that's left to do when shammed
Put all your trust in God, not man

Stop fretting, worring, just de-stress
Because God always gives us his best

A lesson beholden to keep
For I am no longer a little lost sheep

Better, stronger my faith in the Lord
Who knows and controls everything from above

He gives us peace, joy, and mercy
For this I'm thankful forever grateful

"FAIL FORWARD"

When you try and it doesn't work out.
Fail Forward

Never allow your efforts to be in vain
Fail Forward

Pick yourself up, don't look back.
Fail Forward

Start over with a new end in sight
Fail Forward

Savor the best from what was left
Fail Forward

Watch what happens when you persist
Fail Forward

No shame no regret, just figure out what you do best
Fail Forward

///BOGGLED***MIND///

So much is going on, getting hard to keep up.
What is one to do with all this stuff?

Wars, politics, tornados, hurricanes and floods, no love its rough.
All over the world, is it ever going to be enough?

On TV, in the newspapers, and our own backyards.
No matter what we do its difficult to keep up our guards.

The one thing we have to hold on to.
Our relationship with God, me and you.

He covers us both day and night.
Above the clouds out of our sight

We haven't enough eyes to see.
The protection he says I will give to thee.

So keeping all of this in mind.
Is our fathers promising sign.

We don't have to worry or stress.
What he has for us is his best.

Peace, joy, salvation and love.
Holding us in his hands like a tight fitting glove.

WHO ARE YOU?

Who are you?
I Thought I Knew

Then One Day
Out of the Blue

A Different Personality
That Made Me Face Reality

Your Voice was Loud and Clear
The Things I Started to Hear

Frightened me to be near You
I Don't Have a Clue
Is What I'm Hearing True?

It Sounds Cold and Malicious
The Look on Your Face Conspicuous

Saying You Would Harm, Mane and Destroy
As if it's OK

This is Not God's Way
The Things You Say

So Think Again
We're so Near the End

To Lift Our Head in Hell
Is a Permanent Jail

PURPOSE

YOUR LIFE HAS PURPOSE
GOD ALREADY KNEW

WHO YOU ARE
AND WHAT YOU WOULD BE

HE CREATED YOU FOR A CAUSE
ON PURPOSE, NOT EVEN A PAUSE

GO ON AND LET YOUR LIGHT SHINE
VERY SOON YOU WILL FIND

THE PEACE LOVE AND JOY
HE HAS FOR YOU AND MORE

P = Perfect (God's image)
U = Uplifting (above it all)
R = Redemption (saved from sin)
P = Purpose (God has for us)
O = "O" God (Feeling and Emotion)
S = Spirit (God within us)
E = Emmanuel (God with us)

KEEP STRIFE OUT

God rewards you when you do right
The key to happiness is keeping strife out

Honor your spouse
To have calm in your house

You don't have to be right
Let unity win the fight

Put your ego down
Along with the frown

What we model in our home
teaches our children to get along

Show love from your heart
Then peace and joy will never part

NO WISDOM NO VICTORY

A central theme of God's word
Knowledge that must be heard

Understanding that it's true
Is what he expects of me and you

Knowing the way we live is right
Pleasing in his sight

Stedfast, unmovable, lasting
Submission, prayer, fasting

Wisdom does not operate in extremes
Or exaggerated made up dreams

Balance, common sense and good judgement
Falling on our knees in repentance

For God has the last say
Everything will go his way

REPENTANCE OF SIN

Rejoicing in the Lord
Giving him praise

Believing on his word
Renewing of strength

Basking in his glory
Pleasing in his sight

Walk in humble submission
Eager to do his will

Teach total truths
Pleasuring in righteousness

Repentance of sin
Yields great rewards in the end

"TAMING THE TONGUE"

The tongue is a little member
That can do a lot of harm

It can boast great things
A tiny spark can set a blaze

The tongue is a fire, evil and poison
That can be controlled by no man

The tongue is undisciplined
Wild, doing its own thing

We need the help of the Holy Spirit
God will not do it all for us

Take control of it ourselves
Know that, all things are possible

Take the word of God
Speak it over your life

There is power in Words
Negative and Positive

WHY

Is this a question that should be asked?
Maybe the weak, but not the just

For only the just shall see God
The rest walking on crowded, wide sod

That leads to destruction
To late to start new construction

Disregarded the narrow path, with only a few
Not understanding what they knew

God is on the way back for his own
He will not be coming alone

The arch angel will be there with his sword
Taking orders from our Lord

To slay the sinners who did not listen
Not from afar but a very close distance

They to will ascend to meet their master
To take them to his under ground castle

You may not believe this story is true
But, I would give it a second thought if I were you

My God said in his word
He's coming back don't be afraid

Will you be ready when he comes?
Not all are going only some

I plan to be in that number
Awake and ready from my slumber

PLEASING GOD

Tire not of doing good
He shaped us in his image that we would

Share your blessings with others
Bringing joy as you move further

Toward eternal life in Heaven
Singing, praising twenty four, seven

Living in obedience to his word, decreed
With such sacrifices God is pleased

Oh how wonderful it will be
Our father, Jesus, the Angels we'll see

Pain and sickness will be no more
Perfect, full of joy

This life on Earth completely done
A life time in Heaven, the battle won

REFRAME

Sometimes its best to just reframe
Close your lips and not place blame

In your mind imagine a game
So no one will be put to shame

Something's are not worthy of reply
Hold your tongue let out a sigh

Especially when its a lie
And all you can do is wonder why

On the inside feeling dry
On the outside starting to cry

Cringing at the thought it brings
Be strong and think of other things

CREATION

We are created in God's image
To look and act like him every minute

To be imitators of him
and follow his examples, all of them

Speaking things into existance
As though they are already here, be persistant

He has foretold and promised us
All things we need, if we just trust

In Jesus name we must pray
Keep the faith and never stray

LET JESUS TAKE THE WHEEL

Allowing Jesus to take the wheel
Is the greatest Love that you can feel

He leads and guides us on our way
So on the narrow path we stay

There are those who don't understand
The peace and joy of holding his hand

An awesome gift that we possess
If only we trust him and confess

He died that we might live
And gave us all free will

At times we might slip and fall
He's right there to catch us through it all

A Love he gives, that's like no other
To every sister and every brother

Salvation given to the entire world
Because of how much he cares

I RULE OVER THE ENEMY

God gives us the power
To stand strong and tower

Chosen, annointed
Assigned, appointed

To war in the spirit
Not in the flesh

To recognize the stronghold
That satan seeks to unfold

Eyes wide open, sword and shield
Just remember its God's holy will

So enemy move out of the way
You've been defeated depart and stay

No room for you in my life
The world is full of enough trouble and strife

MASTER YOUR FEELINGS

Speaking before thinking
Can result in sinking

Master your feelings
To alleviate healing

Take time to breathe
In order to achieve

Be patient and kind
Let your holy light shine

Even when others
Are revealing their struggles

As long as you know
They just helped you grow

QUESTIONS

Why is life so unfair?
A question in the air

Why are people so unkind?
A question that blows my mind

Why so much doubt, worry and fear?
When God is always near

Why is there so much sin?
When we know we can't win

We can choose to do what's right
The option is in our sight

Why live this way?
All we have to do is pray

Father please guide our feet
So in heaven we all can meet

To live eternally and free
God has given us all a key

DARE TO BELIEVE

- Don't be deceived
- Dare to believe
- Stop to conceive
- What you can achieve
- Get ready to receive
- Know you will succeed
- He knows what you need
- If you dare to believe

CLOSED DOORS

When God closes a door
He opens a window

He loves us more
Than we deserve

Some things our Father blocks
To protect us from ourselves

He knows our hearts and minds
We are his perfect designs

Created in his image
Without a scar or blemish

So stop looking back
You aren't going that way

He said in his holy word
I know the plans I have for you
Loving you is what I do

WHEN GOD IS SILENT

When God is silent
Don't despair he's still there

It may seem
It's the end of your dream

But God's ways are not our ways
He promised to be with us all of our days

One day to him is as a thousand years
Don't get bitter shed no tears

Just keep the faith
Never cease to pray

God hears your call
He answers them all

In his own time
We're always on his mind

IN THE MIDST OF THEM

Where two or three come together
God is in the midst

Believing and trusting in him
Comes at no risk

Whether in times of trouble
Or giving him thanks and praise

We were created to lift his name
All of our living days

To God be the glory
The end of the earthly story

Great is our reward in heaven
Where we will worship him forever

THIRST NO MORE

Jesus confessed I thirst
He came to quench the world

God gives us thirst to remind us
Nothing works without water

Thirst in the flesh is never quenched
We're drenched yet unfulfilled

We must fulfill a spiritual thirst
Through Jesus - a well of living water

Drink of the water that Jesus drinks
And you shall thirst no more

WITH ALL BOLDNESS

Stand boldly without fear
Speak boldly for all to hear

In boldness there is power
To be courageous, firm to tower

Daring confidently and pure
Empowered and strong for sure

No more hesitation or aggravation
Steadfast with prayer and supplication

By the spirit utterance is given
Boldly prevailing to eternal living

Having boldly reached the finish
Ready to start a new beginning

GOD DEFINES ME

I am defined
Specifically designed

God created me with all I need
To carry out my instructed deed

Listen and be still
To do the master's will

I came to fulfill a purpose
A good steward, inside and on the surface

A yearning deep inside
To do my best, while I'm alive

Working toward my assignment everyday
As God continues to direct my way

There is a mark that I will leave
Because my destiny was achieved

DEFEATING THE ENEMY

At the name of Jesus
The enemy will flee

God gives us power
For all to see

Call on his name
Make the enemy ashame

He is no match
For what we've got

Shout Jesus, Jesus
The enemy will leave us

He is afraid
Of those who are saved

PRAYER IS A POWERFUL WEAPON

Pray and believe
And you shall receive

That's what the Bible says
Strengthens you in all your ways

Before you let the devil win
Go back and pray again

By all means
Know that prayer fixes things

- Keep praying don't stop praying

Prayer is a powerful weapon
There's absolutely no exception

Keep praying don't stop praying

NEVER BREAK

We will never break
Although we make mistakes

We will never break
No matter what it takes

We will never break
Through pain, tears and aches

We will never break
For our own sakes

*We - Will - Never - BREAK

We are strong and wonderfully made
Trying to survive in these wicked days

When times are rough
We have to be tough

Enough is enough
Putting up with so much stuff

We - Will - Never - BREAK

BLESSED

No matter what we go through
God already knew

One thing still remains the same
He keeps on blessing us in Jesus name

Giving us continous strength
To accomplish why we were sent

His purpose shall be fulfilled
We need only to stay still

Study his word, the directions
Which gives us connections
Until the resurrection

AN UNCLOUDY DAY

An uncloudy day
Is coming your way

If on this Christian
Journey you stay

It may seem hard
At the start

Just don't give up
When things get tough

Keep trusting and believing
If your plan is receiving

What God has for you
Is for you
No matter what you do

THE GIFT

He died that we all might live.
What an awesome gift to give.

God gave his only begotten son.
His greatest love and it is done.

In return for our life.
There is a continuous fight.

To live for God and give him praise.
To honor him in all our ways.

Undeserving as we might be.
He gives us plen-teous mercy.

It won't be easy my God said.
I give you strength through my word.

Spend a little time with me each day.
To help you find and know the way.

Talk to me in daily prayer and believe.
I promise whatever you need you shall receive.

Through obedience you're one day see my face.
Until then I give you love, peace, protection and grace.

WE WILL BE HEARD

We will be heard
That's what the bible said

Ask and it shall be given
Because my son has risen

He pleds on our behalf
On the cross he bled

That we might have the right
To live an abundant life

On earth as it is in heaven
Where we can live forever

No sickness no pain
No worry or shame

Everything to gain
In Jesus name

BECAUSE I CAN

(Dedicated to Dwight Franklin)

I live a Godly life
Because I can

The kind of life designed
For each and every man

Because I can
It's in God's plan

I choose to love my neighbor
Just one of God's commands

I live a life of righteousness
Because I can

Nothing is impossible
God is in command

I read his word and give him praise
Because I can

LOVE CONQUERS HATE

All Lives Matter

Love conquers hate
It's not up for debate

As sure as God made man
Love is a given command

An emotional feeling
That brings about healing

A feeling of peace
With so much relief

I AGAPE you
And nothing you can do

To change this fact
No taking it back

Love and be loved
God sends it from above

EARLY MORNING

I rise each morning
To see God's glory
I live to tell another story

Everyday brings about change
Nothing again will be the same
How grateful I am in Jesus name

I could have been asleep
In a cold, cold grave
God showed up and I was saved

Still here another day
To bow my head and pray
He's powerful and has his way

Thank you Lord for all you do
I'm safe and secure
Of this I'm sure

WORDS

Words can make you feel good
Words can make you feel bad

Words can make you happy
Words can make you sad

Words can make you fearful
Words can make you glad

Words can be grueling
Words can be soothing

So use words as you should
For the ultimate good

Remember God is listening
Even the words you're whispering

THE BEST IS YET TO COME

The battle has been won.
The best is yet to come.

It seems earth's comforts today have ceased.
Lean on God he gives us peace.

Look up beyond the shadows drear.
And feel his/her presence oh so near.

The time we had.
The memories shared.
Leaves our heart forever glad.

An angel now in heaven above.
He/She touched us deeply with his/her love.

Now rest my sweet, in the fathers arms.
For the best is yet to come.

FINALLY I GET IT

We all start life with a clean slate
A journey thats short and full of mistakes

It takes us years to figure out
What our purpose is all about

Life is about so much more
Surprises, miracles, mysteries galore

Blessings, pain, sometimes even shame
Leaving us wondering who to blame

Family, friends, or maybe ourself
Trying to imagine whats really left

The most important thing, we fail to understand
A relationship we need to have with the man

Our Father who reigns in Heaven above
Who fills our hearts and minds with love

To be successful and fulfilled
Move out of carnal into whats real

Jesus is the answer that we all need
To realize our purpose and do good deeds

Then, comes peace, happiness and joy
The master tells us; go and sin no more

Our sinful lives all erased
Because of Gods unfailing Grace

SEVEN

Number of Completion

1.) Concluded
2.) Finished
3.) Attained
4.) Fulfilled
5.) Realized
6.) Achieved
7.) Finalized

To God Be The Glory
Completes the story

MY PRECIOUS PRINCE

Sometimes life is so unfair
Evil and wickedness everywhere

It shouldn't happen to little ones
Our precious little daughters and sons

But our God said in his word
Loud and clear to be heard

Suffer little children come unto me
He will always keep his hand on thee

The love of God I taught to you
His promise is to see you through

I love you more than words can say
A good life for you each day I pray

My daily prayer is to see you soon
You always have an open room

G'G'

ABOUT THE AUTHOR

Dorris Owney Jackson was born to Samuel Owney Sr. and Maggie Lowe Owney. Number nine of ten children. Attended school in CP Coleman and Watson Chapel school districts. Retired Licensed Practical Nurse. Attended nursing school in Chicago Illinois. Where she lived for many years before returning to Arkansas in 1987. Nursing Career expanded over forty three years. Birth Mother of two a son Cedrick and a daughter Erica. Stepson Preston. Six grandchildren. Great grandson Prince Amir (my heart). Writing Poems goes back seventeen years sharing them with family and friends, with the intention of publishing a book one day. By the grace of God it has been awarded. Writing poems brought about peace and calm in every situation, intensifying the desire to write them as a source of healing. Which absolutely worked. And prayerfully will bring peace and joy to you. Her goal is to encourage and inspire others not to ever lose hope in any situation that life hands them. For truly life is not always fair But God!!! Her poems are true to heart from many experiences in her life. Written during those times. Wherever you are in your life, be assured that when times are tough, when nothing makes sense, when wondering why, and there does not seem to be an answer life is still good. Writing has been a highlight in her life as well as a part of destiny given by God who fulfills and accomplishes every purpose and plan in his heart. This book of Poems felt like a mission to share them with the world. It is exhilarating and heart warming to see them in print. There certainly may be more to come. Remember: All things work together for good to those who Love the LORD and have been called to his purpose. Romans 8:28 TO GOD BE THE GLORY FOR ALL HE HAS DONE.

*My poems are written from the heart
Prayerfully they will encourage and inspire
everyone who reads them.
When we are weak, we are strong
Realizing that life is full of struggles and uncertainties.
May they give you a little more strength to push further.
May you be truly blessed
Truly God is the author
And finisher of our faith*

--Dorris Owney Jackson